Dolch
Sight Word Activities

By Carol Marinovich

Volume 2

SPECTRUM

Grand Rapids, Michigan

Edited by Linda Hartley
Designed by Vicki Langeliers
Illustrated by Larry Brown

Frank Schaffer Publications®

Printed in the United States of America. All rights reserved. Limited Reproduction Permission: Permission
to duplicate these materials is limited to the person for whom they are purchased. Reproduction for an
entire school or school district is unlawful and strictly prohibited. Frank Schaffer Publications is an imprint
of School Specialty Publishing. Copyright © 2003 School Specialty Publishing.

Send all inquiries to:
Frank Schaffer Publications
3195 Wilson Drive NW
Grand Rapids, Michigan 49544

ISBN 1-56189-918-6

6 7 8 9 10 11 12 VHG 09 08 07 06 05

Dolch
Sight Word Activities
Volume 2

Purpose

Dolch Sight Word Activities, Volumes 1 and 2 provide a systematic and sequential method for teaching children the 220 Dolch basic sight words that are needed for a successful experience in beginning reading. *Volume 1* covers 110 of the words in the list and *Volume 2* covers the rest of the words in the list.

The lessons provided in these volumes are designed for quality parent/teacher-student interaction. It is important that you preview with the children the words to be learned prior to the written assignment. This will insure that the children will recognize each word that they are reading and writing.

Each unit introduces a set of five words from the Dolch Sight Words list. The words are presented and reviewed in a consistent way.

Each unit consists of six lessons. The first lesson in the unit introduces the five words by allowing children to trace over the letters. The second lesson allows the children to match words beginning with upper-case letters to the same words beginning with lower-case letters and also to read sentences containing the new words, then draw pictures about the sentences to demonstrate comprehension. The third lesson focuses on recognizing the letters in the words. In the fourth lesson, the children fill in the letters that are missing in the words. In the fifth lesson, children practice sentence completion skills, and the sixth lesson provides children with the opportunity to utilize the new words that they have learned in a meaningful context. An award certificate is supplied at the end of the book. This award certificate provides positive student reinforcement at the completion of this workbook.

Vocabulary Selection

The *Dolch Sight Word Activities Workbooks* use the classic Dolch list of 220 basic vocabulary words that make up from 50% to 75% of all reading matter that children ordinarily encounter. Since these words are ordinarily recognized on sight, they are called *sight words*. *Volume 1* includes 110 sight words. *Volume 2* covers the remainder of the list. Since very few nouns are included in the Dolch list of 220 basic vocabulary words, certain nouns from the Dolch 95 Common Nouns List are added to provide a more meaningful context.

Lesson Instructions
Letter Tracing

Point to the first word in dark print. Read the word to the child and spell the word, pointing to each letter as you say it. Then repeat the word. Finally, have the child trace over the word with a pencil.

If the word is in a sentence, read the sentence to the child. Have the child repeat the sentence. Then ask the child to read the word again. Have the child say each letter in the word as you point to it. Then have the child trace over the word.

Praise the child if the word and letters are said correctly. If a child has difficulty, repeat the activity until the child can read the word.

Repeat this procedure for each of the next four words. Finish the lesson by reviewing all of the words introduced in the worksheet. Do this by pointing at random to each word and asking the child to read the word.

Matching and Visualization

Have the child draw a line to match each word beginning with an upper-case letter to the same word beginning with a lower-case letter.

Then ask the child to read the first sentence over the box aloud. Talk with the child about a picture that could go with that sentence. Using crayons, have the child draw a picture that shows what the sentence is about.

Continue this procedure with the other sentence. When the child has finished drawing, have the child reread both sentences and tell about the pictures.

Scrambled Words

Ask the child to read the first word on the page. Then have the child think of a sentence using that word. Have the child copy the word on the line beside it.

To reinforce the letters that make up the word and to review alphabetical skills, have the child cut out the letters at the bottom of the page and match the letters to the letters in the word being studied. The child can then glue the word onto this line over the printed letters.

Repeat this procedure for the other words on the worksheet unless you find that the child can do the activity independently. If this is the case, have the child read the words aloud to you after completion of the page.

If you wish, you can have the child simply copy the words on the lines instead of cutting them out.

Missing Letters

Point to the word at the top of each section and have the child repeat it after you. If a child has difficulty reading the words, review the words with the child individually.

Then ask the child to write the missing letters for each of the words.

Sentence Completion

If the child is still experiencing difficulty in remembering any of the words, review the words prior to the written work. Use the procedures described in the preceding lessons.

Tell the child to read the words in the box and then read each incomplete sentence. Ask the child to find the word from the box that makes each sentence complete and write it in the blank.

Then ask the child to read the sentences aloud.

Oral Reading/Parent Participation

Tell the child to read the new words in sentences. Then ask the child to read the sentences aloud. Pronounce any words that the child has trouble with.

Student Award

Present the child with an award certificate upon completion of the workbook. The award certificate is located at the end of this book.

The child can color the certificate and display it.

Dolch **Sight Word Activities**

Name _____

Directions: Tell the children, "Read the word that goes with each picture. Then say its letters. Repeat the word. Now trace the word with your pencil."

draw

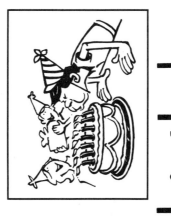

cake

birthday

birthday

Directions: Tell the children, "Read each sentence below. Say the new word printed in dark print. Then say its letters. Repeat the word. Now trace the word with your pencil."

I **wish** my birthday was today.   wish

The birthday cake is **pretty**.   pretty

Dalch **Sight Word Activities**

Name _____

Directions: Tell the children, "Draw a line from each word that begins with a capital letter to the same word that begins with a small letter."

Wish   pretty

Draw   wish

Cake   birthday

Pretty   draw

Birthday   cake

My birthday
is today.

[ ]

I can draw a
big brown monkey.

[ ]

Directions: Tell the children, "Read each sentence. Draw a picture that shows what the sentence is about."

Dolch **Sight Word Activities**

Name _____

wish _____

cake _____

pretty _____

birthday _____

draw _____

a	a	a	b	c	d	d	e	e	h	h	i	i
k	p	r	r	r	s	t	t	t	w	w	y	y

Directions: Tell the children, "Copy each of the words on the line next to the word."

Optional Activity: Tell the children, "Cut out the letters at the bottom of the page. Use the letters to make the words. Then glue each word on the line beside the printed word."

Dolch Sight Word Activities

Name _____

cake

___ ___

___ ak

c ___ e

draw

___ ___

dr ___

___ aw

wish

___ sh

wi ___

pretty

___ ___

___ etty

pre ___ y

birthday

bir ___ day

___ rthday

Directions: Tell the children, "Say each word printed in dark type. Fill in the missing letters."

Dolch **Sight Word Activities**

Name _____

birthday
draw
wish
cake
pretty

1. The _____ girl was in a play at school.

2. I am going to eat my birthday _____ .

3. What do you wish for on your _____ ?

4. Does the girl _____ for a book for her birthday?

5. I can _____ a funny monkey on the grass in the rain.

Directions: Tell the children, "Read the words in dark print. Then read the incomplete sentences. Find the word in dark print that correctly completes each sentence. Then write that word in the blank."

Dolch **Sight Word Activities**

Name _____

PARENTS: Listen to your child read the sentences on this page and put a check mark beside each sentence that is read without error. Then display the paper in a prominent place. If your child has difficulty with any sentence, read the sentence to the child, pointing to each word as you read. Ask the child to read the sentence in the same way. Repeat this procedure several times.

I would like a ball
and a little brown puppy
for my birthday.

"I can draw a monkey
that will look pretty
funny," said the girl.

My wish is to have
my birthday with my
mother and father.

I am going to draw a
pretty white house with
grass around it.

Can you help me cut
this pretty white
birthday cake?

It will get pretty
cold on my birthday.

Directions: Tell the children, "Learn to read the sentences, then take them home to read to your parents."

Dolch **Sight Word Activities**

Name _____

Directions: Tell the children, "Read each sentence below. Say the new word printed in dark print. Then say its letters. Repeat the word. Now trace the word with your pencil."

I wish I **could** play with that cat.   could

She will come **by** today for some cake. by

Put it there **so** he will find it. so

Directions: Tell the children, "Read the word that goes with each picture. Then say its letters. Repeat the word. Now trace the word with your pencil."

fish

fish

man

man

Dolch **Sight Word Activities**

Name

Directions: Tell the children, "Draw a line from each word that begins with a capital letter to the same word that begins with a small letter."

Fish

By

Man

So

Could

so

fish

could

man

by

The man will eat fish.

Could a fish ride in a bus?

Directions: Tell the children, "Read each sentence. Draw a picture that shows what the sentence is about."

Dolch **Sight Word Activities**

Name _____

man _____

by _____

so _____

could _____

fish _____

a	b	c	d	f	i	h	l	m
n	o	o	s	s	u	y		

Directions: Tell the children, "Copy each of the words on the line next to the word."

Optional Activity: Tell the children, "Cut out the letters at the bottom of the page. Use the letters to make the words. Then glue each word on the line beside the printed word."

Dolch **Sight Word Activities**

Name _____

fish

is ___

f _ _ _ h

could

cou ___

c _____ ld

by

man

_ a _

m ___

so

Directions: Tell the children, "Say each word printed in dark type. Fill in the missing letters."

Dolch **Sight Word Activities**

Name _____

so
man
by
could
fish

1. Is this man going to _ _ _ _ _ _ _ _ _ in the rain?

2. The monkey ran _ _ _ _ _ _ _ _ _ our house.

3. The _ _ _ _ _ _ _ _ _ said he was hot.

4. I wish I _ _ _ _ _ _ _ _ _ write a book about a monkey.

5. Can you draw the house _ _ _ _ _ _ _ _ _ that it will look old?

Directions: Tell the children, "Read the words in dark print. Then read the incomplete sentences. Find the word in dark print that correctly completes each sentence. Then write that word in the blank."

Dolch **Sight Word Activities**

Name _____

PARENTS: Listen to your child read the sentences on this page and put a check mark beside each sentence that is read without error. Then display the paper in a prominent place. If your child has difficulty with any sentence, read the sentence to the child, pointing to each word as you read. Ask the child to read the sentence in the same way. Repeat this procedure several times.

The man found the cat going after the fish in the can.

☐ Could a fish play ball with its father in the rain?

Ask my father if we could all fish with him by the old house.

☐ My mother is so pretty that we will have the man draw her.

☐ Could the man and I fish today?

☐ We went by the school so that we could look for the little puppy.

Directions: Tell the children, "Learn to read the sentences, then take them home to read to your parents."

Dalch **Sight Word Activities**

Name _____

Directions: Tell the children, "Read each sentence below. Say the new word printed in dark print. Then say its letters. Repeat the word. Now race the word with your pencil."

I eat cake **when** I have a birthday.

when

I ride the bus by **myself**.

myself

The **old** man will sleep in the chair.

old

Could you **be** in the play with me?

be

Directions: Tell the children, "Read the word that goes with the picture. Then say its letters. Repeat the word. Now trace the word with your pencil."

fly

fly

Dalch **Sight Word Activities**

Name _____

Directions: Tell the children, "Read each sentence. Draw a picture that shows what the sentence is about."

The old man will take the bus.

A big fly is on the cake.

Directions: Tell the children, "Draw a line from each word that begins with a capital letter to the same word that begins with a small letter."

when

myself

old

fly

be

Be

Fly

Myself

When

Old

Dolch **Sight Word Activities**

Name _____

_____

when _____

_____

myself _____

_____

be _____

_____

old _____

_____

fly _____

b	d	e	e	e	f	f	h	l
l	l	l	m	n	o	s	w	y	y

Directions: Tell the children, "Copy each of the words on the line next to the word."

Optional Activity: Tell the children, "Cut out the letters at the bottom of the page. Use the letters to make the words. Then glue each word on the line beside the printed word."

Dolch **Sight Word Activities**

Name _____

when

___ en

wh ___

fly

___ y

___ l

old

___ l

___ d

be

___ ___ ___

myself

___ self

my ___ lf

Dolch Sight Word Activities

Name _____

be
old
myself
fly
when

1. I can make a cake by _____ _____.

2. I wish I could _____ _____.

3. I will _____ a big old fish in the play.

4. _____ I get home from school, I will help my mother.

5. The _____ cat and the puppy like to sit together.

Directions: Tell the children, "Read the words in dark print. Then read the incomplete sentences. Find the word in dark print that correctly completes each sentence. Then write that word in the blank. Use a capital letter at the beginning of a sentence."

Dolch **Sight Word Activities**

Name _____

PARENTS: Listen to your child read the sentences on this page and put a check mark beside each sentence that is read without error. Then display the paper in a prominent place. If your child has difficulty with any sentence, read the sentence to the child, pointing to each word as you read. Ask the child to read the sentence in the same way. Repeat this procedure several times.

☐ I like to be by myself when I read.

☐ When I get old, I am going to be a mother to a little girl.

☐ Can a monkey fly to your house in a can and eat fish and birthday cake?

☐ Does the old man like to fly out here to see your father?

☐ Could I please help myself to some birthday cake?

☐ When will you be at the bus stop?

Directions: Tell the children, "Learn to read the sentences, then take them home to read to your parents."

Dolch **Sight Word Activities**

Name _____

Directions: Tell the children, "Read the word that goes with each picture. Then say its letters. Repeat the word. Now trace the word with your pencil."

elephant

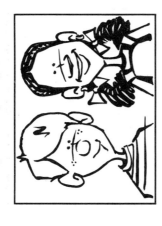

children

squirrel

elephant

children

squirrel

Directions: Tell the children, "Read each sentence below. Say the new word printed in dark print. Then say its letters. Repeat the word. Now trace the word with your pencil."

Is **an** elephant big or little?   an

Children **grow** up fast.   grow

Dolch **Sight Word Activities**

Name _____

Directions: Tell the children, "Draw a line from each word that begins with a capital letter to the same word that begins with a small letter."

Elephant   grow

Squirrel   an

Grow   squirrel

Children   elephant

An   children

The children saw
an elephant
in the grass.

The little squirrel
had some of
my cake.

Directions: Tell the children, "Read each sentence. Draw a picture that shows what the sentence is about."

Dalch Sight Word Activities

Name _____

elephant _____

children _____

squirrel _____

an _____

grow _____

a	a	c	d	e	e	e	e	g	h	h	i	i	l
l	n	n	n	o	p	q	r	r	r	r	s	t	u	w

Directions: Tell the children, "Copy each of the words on the line next to the word."

Optional Activity: Tell the children, "Cut out the letters at the bottom of the page. Use the letters to make the words. Then glue each word on the line beside the printed word."

Dolch **Sight Word Activities**

Name _____

---

elephant

_____ l _____ phant

elepha _____ _____

---

grow

_____ _____ ow

gr _____ _____

---

an

_____ _____ _____

---

squirrel

squi _____ el

s _____ irrel

---

children

_____ ildren

chi _____ ren

Directions: Tell the children, "Say each word printed in dark type. Fill in the missing letters."

Dolch Sight Word Activities

Name _____

an
children
grow
elephant
squirrel

1. _____ _____ elephant can not fly.

2. What will you be when you _____ _____ up?

3. An _____ _____ will not go to school.

4. Could the _____ _____ ride the bus to school today?

5. My mother will not let me play with a _____ .

Directions: Tell the children, "Read the words in dark print. Then read the incomplete sentences. Find the word in dark print that correctly completes each sentence. Then write that word in the blank. Use a capital letter at the beginning of a sentence."

Dolch **Sight Word Activities**

Name _____

PARENTS: Listen to your child read the sentences on this page and put a check mark beside each sentence that is read without error. Then display the paper in a prominent place. If your child has difficulty with any sentence, read the sentence to the child, pointing to each word as you read. Ask the child to read the sentence in the same way. Repeat this procedure several times.

☐ The grass by the school will grow after the rain.

☐ All of the children saw the fast squirrel run around in the grass.

☐ The boy found some cake for the little squirrel to eat.

☐ The little elephant will grow to be a big, big elephant.

☐ "Come with us to help your mother," Father said to the children.

☐ Can an elephant help a squirrel read a book?

Directions: Tell the children, "Learn to read the sentences, then take them home to read to your parents."

Dolch **Sight Word Activities**

Name _____

Directions: Tell the children, "Read the word that goes with each picture. Then say its letters. Repeat the word. Now trace the word with your pencil."

drink

drink

milk

milk

toys

toys

Directions: Tell the children, "Read each sentence below. Say the new word printed in dark print. Then say its letters. Repeat the word. Now trace the word with your pencil."

Can he find **his** toys?   his

Do you know **why** an elephant can not ride on a bus?   why

Dolch **Sight Word Activities**

Name _____

Directions: Tell the children, "Draw a line from each word that begins with a capital letter to the same word that begins with a small letter."

Toys

Why

Milk

His

Drink

drink

his

toys

why

milk

The man will
drink his milk.

The boy will fish
with his father.

Directions: Tell the children, "Read each sentence. Draw a picture that shows what the sentence means."

Dolch Sight Word Activities

Name _____

toys _____

why _____

drink _____

his _____

milk _____

d	h	h	i	i	i	k	k	l	m	n
o	r	s	s	t	w	y	y

Directions: Tell the children, "Copy each of the words on the line next to the word."

Optional Activity: Tell the children, "Cut out the letters at the bottom of the page. Use the letters to make the words. Then glue each word on the line beside the printed word."

***Dolch* Sight Word Activities**

Name

toys

t __ __ y __

__ o __ s

milk

__ __ __

__ __ lk

mi __

drink

dri __ __

__ __ ink

his

__ __ i __

h __ __

why

__ __ y

w __ __

Dolch **Sight Word Activities**

Name _____

milk
drink
his
toys
why

1. Do you know _____ _____ you are at school?

2. A cat will drink _____ _____ your milk so that you will grow.

3. _____ _____ be for the little children?

4. Could the _____ be for the little children?

5. Please thank _____ father for the book about fish.

Directions: Tell the children, "Read the words in dark print. Then read the incomplete sentences. Find the word in dark print that correctly completes each sentence. Then write that word in the blank. Use a capital letter at the beginning of a sentence."

Dolch **Sight Word Activities**

Name _____

The children will draw an elephant that can eat a bus.

Can you tell me why an elephant can grow so big and why a fly can not?

Drink your milk so you can play with your toys.

Why does the boy drink his milk so fast?

Can you tell me why you like to play with toys?

Why are his toys out on the grass in the rain?

Dalch **Sight Word Activities**

Name

Directions: Tell the children, "Read the word that goes with the picture. Then say its letters. Repeat the word. Now trace the word with your pencil."

Directions: Tell the children, "Read each sentence below. Say the new word printed in dark print. Then say its letters. Repeat the word. Now trace the word with your pencil."

The girl **got** toys for her birthday.   got

Is it **better** to be hot or cold?   better

This fish is so **good**, I will eat it all.   good

I will put **these** toys on the chair.   these

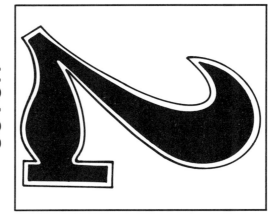

seven

seven

Dolch **Sight Word Activities**

Name _____

Directions: Tell the children, "Draw a line from each word that begins with a capital letter to the same word that begins with a small letter."

Got	good
Better	seven
Seven	got
Good	these
These	better

These children like to laugh.

My seven fish are funny together.

Directions: Tell the children, "Read each sentence. Draw a picture that shows what the sentence means."

Dolch **Sight Word Activities**

Name _____

_____

these _____

seven _____

good _____

got _____

better _____

b	d	e	e	e	e	e	g	g	h	n	o
o	o	r	s	s	t	t	t	v

Directions: Tell the children, "Copy each of the words on the line next to the word."

Optional Activity: Tell the children, "Cut out the letters at the bottom of the page. Use the letters to make the words. Then glue each word on the line beside the printed word."

Dolch **Sight Word Activities**

Name _____

better

be___er

___tter

got

___t

g___

good

g___

___oo d

these

the___

___ese

seven

s___v___n

e___en

Dolch **Sight Word Activities**

Name _____

better
good
these
got
seven

1. Milk is _____ _____ to drink with cake.

2. _____ _____ fish are good and hot.

3. "I had _____ get that fly," said Father.

4. _____ _____ children have got to do better in school.

5. We _____ our wish to keep all of the toys.

Directions: Tell the children, "Read the words in dark print. Then read the incomplete sentences. Find the word in dark print that correctly completes each sentence. Then write that word in the blank. Use a capital letter at the beginning of a sentence."

Dolch **Sight Word Activities**

Name _____

PARENTS: Listen to your child read the sentences on this page and put a check mark beside each sentence that is read without error. Then display the paper in a prominent place. If your child has difficulty with any sentence, read the sentence to the child, pointing to each word as you read. Ask the child to read the sentence in the same way. Repeat this procedure several times.

☐ These seven children are good and kind to the old cat.

☐ I can draw a squirrel, but these children can draw one better.

☐ The milk is good, but the hot fish is better.

☐ I had better be going so that I can get to school before seven.

☐ These seven children ate seven fish that were good and hot.

☐ The old man got better after his sleep.

Directions: Tell the children, "Learn to read the sentences, then take them home to read to your parents."

Dolch **Sight Word Activities**

Name _____

Directions: Tell the children, "Read the word that goes with the picture. Then say its letters. Repeat the word. Now trace the word with your pencil."

Directions: Tell the children, "Read each sentence below. Say the new word printed in dark print. Then say its letters. Repeat the word. Now trace the word with your pencil."

Will that old school bus **start**?

start

Today is his **first** birthday.

first

Who is the man with my father?

who

The **blue** house is by the school.

blue

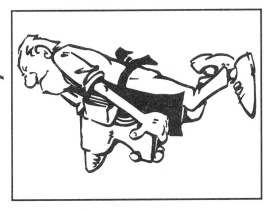

carry

carry

Dolch **Sight Word Activities**

Name _____

Directions: Tell the children, "Draw a line from each word that begins with a capital letter to the same word that begins with a small letter."

first

start

carry

who

blue

Who

Carry

Blue

Start

First

There is a blue light by that old house.

An elephant can carry a brown monkey.

Directions: Tell the children, "Read each sentence. Draw a picture that shows what the sentence means."

Unit 32

Scrambled Words 3

Dolch **Sight Word Activities**

Name _____

carry _____

start _____

who _____

blue _____

first _____

a	a	b	c	e	f	h	i	i	l	o	r
r	r	r	s	s	t	t	t	t	u	w	y

Directions: Tell the children, "Copy each of the words on the line next to the word."

Optional Activity: Tell the children, "Cut out the letters at the bottom of the page. Use the letters to make the words. Then glue each word on the line beside the printed word."

Dolch **Sight Word Activities**

Name _____

who

_____ o

w _____

carry

ca _____ y

_____ rry

start

_____ tar

sta _____

first

_____ rst

fir _____

blue

_____ ue

bl _____

Directions: Tell the children, "Say each word printed in dark type. Fill in the missing letters."

Dolch **Sight Word Activities**

Name _____

blue
who
carry
start
first

1. Who will be _____ _ _ _ to drink his milk?

2. Today I will _____ _ _ _ going to school.

3. That chair is _ _ _ _ _____ and brown.

4. Do you know _____ _ _ _ will carry all of these toys?

5. Could the man _____ _ _ _ the puppy to our house?

Directions: Tell the children, "Read the words in dark print. Then read the incomplete sentences. Find the word in dark print that correctly completes each sentence. Then write that word in the blank."

Dalch **Sight Word Activities**

Name _____

PARENTS: Listen to your child read the sentences on this page and put a check mark beside each sentence that is read without error. Then display the paper in a prominent place. If your child has difficulty with any sentence, read the sentence to the child, pointing to each word as you read. Ask the child to read the sentence in the same way. Repeat this procedure several times.

☐ Who has a blue ball
we can play with?

☐ You can start to draw
a white cat going after
a blue fish.

☐ Carry the fish and milk
over here so we can
start to eat.

☐ A blue elephant and
a blue monkey would
not be pretty.

☐ The blue bus will be
the first to take an
elephant for a ride.

☐ Who will carry
the big blue book
to the bus stop?

Directions: Tell the children, "Learn to read the sentences, then take them home to read to your parents."

Dolch **Sight Word Activities**

Name _____

Directions: Tell the children, "Read the word that goes with each picture. Then say its letters. Repeat the word. Now trace the word with your pencil."

Directions: Tell the children, "Read each sentence below. Say the new word printed in dark print. Then say its letters. Repeat the word. Now trace the word with your pencil."

Will **any** of you sing to me?

city

I **hurt** myself in the water.

hurt

Never carry an elephant.

Never

table

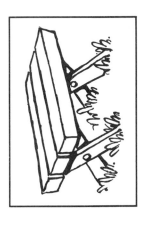

table

water

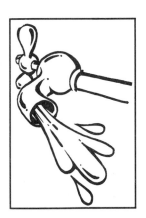

water

Name _____

Directions: Tell the children, "Draw a line from each word that begins with a capital letter to the same word that begins with a small letter."

Never

Water

Hurt

Any

Table

hurt

any

table

water

never

The blue book is
on the table.

The fish are
in the water.

Directions: Tell the children, "Read each sentence. Draw a picture that shows what the sentence means."

Dolch Sight Word Activities

Name _____

water _____

never _____

table _____

any _____

hurt _____

a	a	a	b	e	e	e	e	h	n
n	r	r	r	t	t	t	u	v	w	y

Directions: Tell the children, "Copy each of the words on the line next to the word."

Optional Activity: Tell the children, "Cut out the letters at the bottom of the page. Use the letters to make the words. Then glue each word on the line beside the printed word."

Dolch **Sight Word Activities**

Name _____

when

nev ___ ___

n ___ er

hurt

h ___ ___ t

___ ur ___

never

___ he ___

w ___ ___ n

table

___ ___ ble

tab ___ ___

water

wa ___ ___ r

___ ___ ter

Directions: Tell the children, "Say each word printed in dark type. Fill in the missing letters."

Dolch Sight Word Activities

Name _____

never
hurt
any
table
water

1. You would _ _ _ _ _ _ _ _ hurt a puppy.

2. Put all of his toys on the _ _ _ _ _ _ _ _ .

3. Do you _ _ _ _ _ _ _ _ after you run fast?

4. Would _ _ _ _ _ _ _ _ of you like to water the grass for me?

5. Cold _ _ _ _ _ _ _ _ will get in the old house after the rain.

Directions: Tell the children, "Read the words in dark print. Then read the incomplete sentences. Find the word in dark print that correctly completes each sentence. Then write that word in the blank."

Dolch **Sight Word Activities**

Name _____

PARENTS: Listen to your child read the sentences on this page and put a check mark beside each sentence that is read without error. Then display the paper in a prominent place. If your child has difficulty with any sentence, read the sentence to the child, pointing to each word as you read. Ask the child to read the sentence in the same way. Repeat this procedure several times.

☐ I hurt myself today when I got a cut.

☐ Your drink of water and the book I got for you are on the table.

☐ It may be that the bus boy will never put the water on the table.

☐ Kind children would never hurt a little puppy or cat.

☐ We will drink the water that is on the table when we eat our fish.

☐ Who was hurt when going to school?

Directions: Tell the children, "Learn to read the sentences, then take them home to read to your parents."

Dolch **Sight Word Activities**

Name _____

Directions: Tell the children, "Read the word that goes with each picture. Then say its letters. Repeat the word. Now trace the word with your pencil."

Directions: Tell the children, "Read each sentence below. Say the new word printed in dark print. Then say its letters. Repeat the word. Now trace the word with your pencil."

Show the little squirrel to Father.

show

There are **five** fish in the water.

five

Do you have your **own** house?

own

doll

doll

chickens

chickens

Dolch **Sight Word Activities**

Name _____

Directions: Tell the children, "Draw a line from each word that begins with a capital letter to the same word that begins with a small letter."

Five

Doll

Show

Own

Chickens

own

five

chickens

doll

show

I have never had a doll this pretty before.

Are any of these five chickens yours?

Directions: Tell the children, "Read each sentence. Draw a picture that shows what the sentence means."

Name _____

chickens _____ _____   five _____

doll _____ _____   own _____

show _____

c	c	d	e	e	f	h	h	i	i	k	l	l
o	o	o	o	n	n	n	s	s	v	w	w	

Directions: Tell the children, "Copy each of the words on the line next to the word."

Optional Activity: Tell the children, "Cut out the letters at the bottom of the page. Use the letters to make the words. Then glue each word on the line beside the printed word."

Dolch Sight Word Activities

Name _____

five

___ ve

fi ___

doll

d ___ l

___ o ___ l

show

___ ho ___

s ___ w

chickens

chi ___ ens

___ ickens

own

___ n

o ___

Directions: Tell the children, "Say each word printed in dark type. Fill in the missing letters."

Dolch Sight Word Activities

Name _____

| five |
| show |
| **chickens** |
| own |
| doll |

1. My pretty _ _ _ _ _ _ _ has a birthday today.

2. My _____ chickens can not fly.

3. Let me _ _ _ _ _ _ you how to fish.

4. I do not _____ an elephant.

5. Our _ _ _ _ _ _ _ like to run around in the grass.

Directions: Tell the children, "Read the words in dark print. Then read the incomplete sentences. Find the word in dark print that correctly completes each sentence. Then write that word in the blank."

Dolch **Sight Word Activities**

Name _____

PARENTS: Listen to your child read the sentences on this page and put a check mark beside each sentence that is read without error. Then display the paper in a prominent place. If your child has difficulty with any sentence, read the sentence to the child, pointing to each word as you read. Ask the child to read the sentence in the same way. Repeat this procedure several times.

The five chickens may never go in the house.

Mother has an old doll house that she may show us.

Would you show me the chickens that got hurt?

The girl put on her own doll show at school.

I own the five fish over there in the water.

The girl and the boy own five big chickens.

Directions: Tell the children, "Learn to read the sentences, then take them home to read to your parents."

Dolch **Sight Word Activities**

Name _____

Directions: Tell the children, "Read the word that goes with each picture. Then say its letters. Repeat the word. Now trace the word with your pencil."

Directions: Tell the children, "Read each sentence below. Say the new word printed in dark print. Then say its letters. Repeat the word. Now trace the word with your pencil."

You **don't** like fish, do you?

don't

Would you like to **hold** my doll?

hold

The little chickens are **yellow**.

yellow

well

well

walk

walk

Name _____

Directions: Tell the children, "Draw a line from each word that begins with a capital letter to the same word that begins with a small letter."

Don't

Walk

Hold

Yellow

Well

yellow

well

don't

walk

hold

The little yellow chickens can not walk well.

A man can hold five big fish.

Directions: Tell the children, "Read each sentence. Draw a picture that shows what the sentence means."

Dolch Sight Word Activities

Name _____

don't _____

_____ walk

well _____

_____ yellow

hold _____

a	d	d	e	e	h	k	l	l	l	l	l
n	o	o	o	t	w	w	w	y	'		

Directions: Tell the children, "Copy each of the words on the line next to the word."

Optional Activity: Tell the children, "Cut out the letters at the bottom of the page. Use the letters to make the words. Then glue each word on the line beside the printed word."

Dolch **Sight Word Activities**

Name _____

well

we _ _ _

_ _ _ ll

hold

_ _ ol _

h _ _ d

don't

don _ _

_ _ n't

walk

_ _ al _

w _ _ k

yellow

ye _ _ ow

_ _ llow

Dolch **Sight Word Activities**

Name _____

walk
yellow
well
hold
don't

1. We can get cold water at the _____ _ _ _ _ _ .

2. My little chair is brown and _____ _ _ _ _ _ .

3. The boy will _____ _ _ _ _ _ to school today.

4. Chickens _____ _ _ _ _ _ like to play with a monkey.

5. Would you like to _____ _ _ _ _ _ my new little puppy?

Directions: Tell the children, "Read the words in dark print. Then read the incomplete sentences. Find the word in dark print that correctly completes each sentence. Then write that word in the blank."

Dolch Sight Word Activities

Name _____

PARENTS: Listen to your child read the sentences on this page and put a check mark beside each sentence that is read without error. Then display the paper in a prominent place. If your child has difficulty with any sentence, read the sentence to the child, pointing to each word as you read. Ask the child to read the sentence in the same way. Repeat this procedure several times.

☐ Don't show the little cat how to get up on the table.

☐ Mother said, "If you are good, you can hold the brown puppy."

☐ The boy got hurt. He is not well.

☐ We can walk from our house to the old well.

☐ We saw five little yellow chickens by the blue water.

☐ Don't walk when you see a yellow light.

Directions: Tell the children, "Learn to read the sentences, then take them home to read to your parents."

Dolch **Sight Word Activities**

Name _____

Directions: Tell the children, "Read each sentence below. Say the new word printed in dark print. Then say its letters. Repeat the word. Now trace the word with your pencil."

Do the children have to walk **far** to get to school?

far

The table is **green**.

green

The chair is **red**.

red

How far **away** is the little blue house?

away

Hold the puppy so that it will not **fall**.

fall

Dolch **Sight Word Activities**

Name _____

Directions: Tell the children, "Draw a line from each word that begins with a capital letter to the same word that begins with a small letter."

Far

Green

Fall

Away

Red

away

red

far

green

fall

The grass is green by the red school house.

The little squirrel is far away from the old man.

Directions: Tell the children, "Read each sentence. Draw a picture that shows what the sentence means."

Dolch **Sight Word Activities**

Name _____

far _____

fall _____

red _____

green _____

away _____

a	l	l	a	a	d	e	e	e	f	f	g
l	l	n	r	r	r	r	w	y

Directions: Tell the children, "Copy each of the words on the line next to the word."

Optional Activity: Tell the children, "Cut out the letters at the bottom of the page. Use the letters to make the words. Then glue each word on the line beside the printed word."

Dalch Sight Word Activities

Name _____

far

__ a __ __

__ __ r

away

__ __ a y

a w __ __

green

g r __ __ n

__ __ e e n

fall

f __ l l

__ a l __

red

__ __ d

r __ __

Dolch Sight Word Activities

Name _____

away
far
green
fall
red

1. How _____ away is the bus stop?

2. Where is the big _____ ball?

3. These chickens will not fly far _____ .

4. Hold the little doll so that it does not _____ .

5. This yellow grass will be _____ after the rain.

Directions: Tell the children, "Read the words in dark print. Then read the incomplete sentences. Find the word in dark print that correctly completes each sentence. Then write that word in the blank."

Dolch **Sight Word Activities**

Name _____

PARENTS: Listen to your child read the sentences on this page and put a check mark beside each sentence that is read without error. Then display the paper in a prominent place. If your child has difficulty with any sentence, read the sentence to the child, pointing to each word as you read. Ask the child to read the sentence in the same way. Repeat this procedure several times.

☐ My school is red and my school bus is yellow.

☐ My house is far away from my school.

☐ I like to walk to school in the fall when it is hot.

☐ Will that red and green book fall from the table?

☐ Show me how far a squirrel can jump.

☐ Will we have to go far to find the yellow school bus?

Directions: Tell the children, "Learn to read the sentences, then take them home to read to your parents."

Dolch **Sight Word Activities**

Name _____

Directions: Tell the children, "Read the word that goes with the picture. Then say its letters. Repeat the word. Now trace the word with your pencil."

Directions: Tell the children, "Read each sentence below. Say the new word printed in dark print. Then say its letters. Repeat the word. Now trace the word with your pencil."

Please **try** not to fall in the water.   try

An elephant is **very** big.   very

Is the red light **off**?   off

Did the children get **their** wish?   their

call

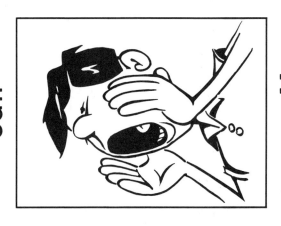

call

Dolch **Sight Word Activities**

Name _____

Directions: Tell the children, "Draw a line from each word that begins with a capital letter to the same word that begins with a small letter."

Try	very
Off	call
Call	their
Very	off
Their	try

The girl will try to call her mother who is far away.

The squirrel can run very far very fast.

Directions: Tell the children, "Read each sentence. Draw a picture that shows what the sentence means."

Dolch **Sight Word Activities**

Name _____

very _____

off _____

call _____

try _____

their _____

a	c	e	e	f	f	h	i	l	l	o
r	r	r	r	t	t	v	y	y		

Directions: Tell the children, "Copy each of the words on the line next to the word."

Optional Activity: Tell the children, "Cut out the letters at the bottom of the page. Use the letters to make the words. Then glue each word on the line beside the printed word."

Dolch **Sight Word Activities**

Name _____

call

___ ll

ca ___

very

v ___ r

___ e ___ y

their

___ t ___ ir

the ___

off

___ f

o ___

try

___ y

t ___

Dolch **Sight Word Activities**

Name _____

call
their
try
off
very

1. Get _ _ _ _ _ _ _ _ that yellow table!

2. _ _ _ _ _ _ _ _ to start the old red bus, please.

3. The girl with the big doll is _ _ _ _ _ _ _ _ pretty.

4. Try to _ _ _ _ _ _ _ _ the children to come in here to eat.

5. Call the children to come and get _ _ _ _ _ _ _ _ toys.

Directions: Tell the children, "Read the words in dark print. Then read the incomplete sentences. Find the word in dark print that correctly completes each sentence. Then write that word in the blank. Use a capital letter at the beginning of a sentence."

Dolch **Sight Word Activities**

Name _____

PARENTS: Listen to your child read the sentences on this page and put a check mark beside each sentence that is read without error. Then display the paper in a prominent place. If your child has difficulty with any sentence, read the sentence to the child, pointing to each word as you read. Ask the child to read the sentence in the same way. Repeat this procedure several times.

☐ Did Mother try to call off their fall show?

Try to get the boy
☐ to carry the green book to school today.

☐ Do we have to call off the play?

☐ Is your birthday very far off?

☐ There is much to eat and drink on their table.

☐ Did you thank the children for their toys?

Directions: Tell the children, "Learn to read the sentences, then take them home to read to your parents."

Dolch **Sight Word Activities**

Name _____

Directions: Tell the children, "Read each sentence below. Say the new word printed in dark print. Then say its letters. Repeat the word. Now trace the word with your pencil."

Tell the children that we like **them** very much.

them

Did **they** go to the show today?

they

Pick up your toys.

Pick

The girl can walk very fast, **but** the boy can not.

but

We will help Mother **clean** the house.

clean

Dolch **Sight Word Activities**

Name _____

Directions: Tell the children, "Draw a line from each word that begins with a capital letter to the same word that begins with a small letter."

The boy will clean off his toys.

The girl got to pick out a new doll.

Directions: Tell the children, "Read each sentence. Draw a picture that shows what the sentence means."

Them	clean
Pick	but
But	they
Clean	pick
They	them

Dolch **Sight Word Activities**

Name _____

pick _____

but _____

clean _____

them _____

they _____

a	b	c	c	e	e	e	h	h	i	k
l	l	m	n	p	t	t	t	u	y

Directions: Tell the children, "Copy each of the words on the line next to the word."

Optional Activity: Tell the children, "Cut out the letters at the bottom of the page. Use the letters to make the words. Then glue each word on the line beside the printed word."

Dolch **Sight Word Activities**

Name _____

them

_____ em

th _____

pick

_____ ic

p _____ k

but

_____ t

_____ b

clean

c _____ ea

cl _____ n

they

th _____

_____ ey

Directions: Tell the children, "Say each word printed in dark type. Fill in the missing letters."

Dolch Sight Word Activities

Name _____

pick
they
but
them
clean

1. We went to the funny show with _ _ _ _ _ _ _ _ _ _ .

2. The boy will _ _ _ _ _ _ _ _ the house for us.

3. The house is old, _ _ _ _ _ _ _ _ it is clean.

4. _ _ _ _ _ _ _ _ up the chair and put it over here by the table.

5. _ _ _ _ _ _ _ _ may come over to hold the puppy.

Directions: Tell the children, "Read the words in dark print. Then read the incomplete sentences. Find the word in dark print that correctly completes each sentence. Then write that word in the blank. Use a capital letter at the beginning of a sentence."

Dolch **Sight Word Activities**

Name _____

PARENTS: Listen to your child read the sentences on this page and put a check mark beside each sentence that is read without error. Then display the paper in a prominent place. If your child has difficulty with any sentence, read the sentence to the child, pointing to each word as you read. Ask the child to read the sentence in the same way. Repeat this procedure several times.

☐ They like to eat fish, but they do not like to clean them.

☐ Father will pick out a table and chair for Mother for her birthday.

☐ They will try not to fall in the water, but some of them will fall in.

☐ Who will pick them up after the show?

☐ The house is clean, but it is very old.

☐ Tell them to pick up the house so it will be clean.

Directions: Tell the children, "Learn to read the sentences, then take them home to read to your parents."

Dolch **Sight Word Activities**

Name _____

Directions: Tell the children, "Read each sentence below. Say the new word printed in dark print. Then say its letters. Repeat the word. Now trace the word with your pencil."

Is the girl up **or** did she go to sleep? or

We **must** clean the house today. must

Would you all get together **now**? now

I like the house **because** it is clean. because

May I go to school, **too**? too

Dolch Sight Word Activities

Name _____

Directions: Tell the children, "Draw a line from each word that begins with a capital letter to the same word that begins with a small letter."

Or

Because

Too

Now

Must

must

now

because

or

too

The little boy must carry his book to school.

The girl got a doll because it is her birthday.

Directions: Tell the children, "Read each sentence. Draw a picture that shows what the sentence means."

Dolch **Sight Word Activities**

Name _____

because _____

_____ now

too _____

_____ must

or _____

a	b	c	e	e	m	n	o	o	o	o
r		s	s	t	t	u	u	w		

Directions: Tell the children, "Copy each of the words on the line next to the word."

Optional Activity: Tell the children, "Cut out the letters at the bottom of the page. Use the letters to make the words. Then glue each word on the line beside the printed word."

Unit 39

Missing Letters 4

Dolch Sight Word Activities

Name _____

must

mu _ _ st

or

_ _ _ _

now

_ n _ o

because

bec _ se

_ cause

too

_ o t

Directions: Tell the children, "Say each word printed in dark type. Fill in the missing letters."

Dolch **Sight Word Activities**

Name _____

because
must
or
now
too

1. We can not play _____ _ _ _ _ of the rain.

2. Did she eat _____ _ _ _ _ much fish?

3. The children _____ _ _ _ _ go to school.

4. You may water the grass _____ _ _ _ _ help your mother.

5. Can you pick up the cake _____ or after school?

Directions: Tell the children, "Read the words in dark print. Then read the incomplete sentences. Find the word in dark print that correctly completes each sentence. Then write that word in the blank."

Dolch **Sight Word Activities**

Name _____

PARENTS: Listen to your child read the sentences on this page and put a check mark beside each sentence that is read without error. Then display the paper in a prominent place. If your child has difficulty with any sentence, read the sentence to the child, pointing to each word as you read. Ask the child to read the sentence in the same way. Repeat this procedure several times.

☐ The house is very clean today because Mother had me pick it up.

☐ We must go now, because we have to walk to the bus stop.

☐ Can there be too much rain or too little rain?

☐ Must we go now or can we go after I see the funny show?

☐ You must go now because my mother will try to call me.

☐ The boy or the girl must help me look for the little yellow book.

Directions: Tell the children, "Learn to read the sentences, then take them home to read to your parents."

Dolch **Sight Word Activities**

Name _____

Directions: Tell the children, "Read the word that goes with each picture. Then say its letters. Repeat the word. Now trace the word with your pencil."

Directions: Tell the children, "Read each sentence below. Say the new word printed in dark print. Then say its letters. Repeat the word. Now trace the word with your pencil."

Can you **pull** the wagon?   pull

Did the boy fall **down**?   down

The wagon is **full** of fish.   full

wagon

wagon
one

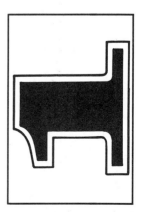

one

Dalch **Sight Word Activities**

Name _____

Directions: Tell the children, "Draw a line from each word that begins with a capital letter to the same word that begins with a small letter."

Wagon

Full

Down

Pull

One

full

pull

one

wagon

down

The girl will pull the wagon full of toys.

The blue wagon has one big, brown squirrel in it.

Directions: Tell the children, "Read each sentence. Draw a picture that shows what the sentence means."

Dolch Sight Word Activities

Name _____

_____

pull

_____

wagon

_____

down

_____

full

_____

one

a	e	d	f	g	l	l	l	l	n	n
n	o	o	o	p	o	p	u	u	w	w

Directions: Tell the children, "Copy each of the words on the line next to the word."

Optional Activity: Tell the children, "Cut out the letters at the bottom of the page. Use the letters to make the words. Then glue each word on the line beside the printed word."

Dolch **Sight Word Activities**

Name _____

one

_____ n _____ _____ e

down

_____ ow _____ d _____ n

pull

_____ ll _____ pu _____ d

full

_____ ll _____ fu _____

wagon

_____ gon _____ wa _____ n

Directions: Tell the children, "Say each word printed in dark type. Fill in the missing letters."

Dalch **Sight Word Activities**

Name _____

wagon
pull
one
down
full

1. After you eat, are you _____ ?

2. _____ boy did not drink his milk.

3. The elephant will _____ the wagon.

4. The little girl got the big red _____ for her birthday.

5. "Put the puppy _____," said Mother.

Directions: Tell the children, "Read the words in dark print. Then read the incomplete sentences. Find the word in dark print that correctly completes each sentence. Then write that word in the blank. Use a capital letter at the beginning of a sentence."

Dolch **Sight Word Activities**

Name _____

PARENTS: Listen to your child read the sentences on this page and put a check mark beside each sentence that is read without error. Then display the paper in a prominent place. If your child has difficulty with any sentence, read the sentence to the child, pointing to each word as you read. Ask the child to read the sentence in the same way. Repeat this procedure several times.

Can you help me
pull this wagon full
of green grass?

One of the children
will have to write down
what you said.

Pull the wagon down
to the water so that
you can clean it.

Pull the red wagon down
to my house so that we
can play with it.

Did one of the chickens
fall down the well?

One of the children
found a pretty little doll
down by the old house.

Directions: Tell the children, "Learn to read the sentences, then take them home to read to your parents."

Dolch **Sight Word Activities**

Name _____

Directions: Tell the children, "Read the word that goes with each picture. Then say its letters. Repeat the word. Now trace the word with your pencil."

Directions: Tell the children, "Read each sentence below. Say the new word printed in dark print. Then say its letters. Repeat the word. Now trace the word with your pencil."

Which book is better?

Which

Can you **use** a chair to sit on?

use

The ring is **round** and pretty.

round

eight

eight

ring

ring

Dolch **Sight Word Activities**

Name _____

Directions: Tell the children, "Draw a line from each word that begins with a capital letter to the same word that begins with a small letter."

Round   which

Use   eight

Eight   use

Ring   round

Which   ring

A big round ring is on the table.

The old man will eat eight fish.

Directions: Tell the children, "Read each sentence. Draw a picture that shows what the sentence means."

Dolch **Sight Word Activities**

Name _____

which _____

use _____

eight _____

ring _____

round _____

c	d	e	e	g	g	h	h	i	i
i	n	n	o	r	r	s	t	u	u	w

Directions: Tell the children, "Copy each of the words on the line next to the word."

Optional Activity: Tell the children, "Cut out the letters at the bottom of the page. Use the letters to make the words. Then glue each word on the line beside the printed word."

Dolch **Sight Word Activities**

Name _____

use

e _ _

_ u _

ring

_ i _ g

r _ n _

eight

ei _ _ t

_ _ ght

round

r _ _ nd

rou _ _

which

w _ i _ h

_ hic _

Directions: Tell the children, "Say each word printed in dark type. Fill in the missing letters."

Dolch Sight Word Activities

Name _____

eight
ring
use
round
which

1. _____ chickens are in the wagon.

2. _____ doll do you like to play with?

3. She got a green _____ for her birthday.

4. Can you _____ that old wagon to get your toys?

5. Why does that boy run round and _____ our house?

Directions: Tell the children, "Read the words in dark print. Then read the incomplete sentences. Find the word in dark print that correctly completes each sentence. Then write that word in the blank. Use a capital letter at the beginning of a sentence."

Dalch **Sight Word Activities**

Name _____

PARENTS: Listen to your child read the sentences on this page and put a check mark beside each sentence that is read without error. Then display the paper in a prominent place. If your child has difficulty with any sentence, read the sentence to the child, pointing to each word as you read. Ask the child to read the sentence in the same way. Repeat this procedure several times.

☐ I know which wagon we can use to get the toys.

☐ A birthday cake and a ring are round. Is a ball round?

☐ Which one of the eight chickens ran away?

☐ Which of the children will Father ask to help him pick out a ring?

☐ Please use your own table to draw on.

☐ Can a ring not be round?

Directions: Tell the children, "Learn to read the sentences, then take them home to read to your parents."

Dolch **Sight Word Activities**

Name _____

Directions: Tell the children, "Read the word that goes with the picture. Then say its letters. Repeat the word. Now trace the word with your pencil."

Directions: Tell the children, "Read each sentence below. Say the new word printed in dark print. Then say its letters. Repeat the word. Now trace the word with your pencil."

Must I clean the house **again**?

again

Do you **want** to go to the cat show?

want

You have **been** a good girl today.

been

Did the chickens get **into** the house?

into

two

two

Dolch **Sight Word Activities**

Name _____

Directions: Tell the children, "Draw a line from each word that begins with a capital letter to the same word that begins with a small letter."

Two

Want

Again

Into

Been

been

into

want

again

two

The chickens want
to eat again.

Two children are
going into the
cold water.

Directions: Tell the children, "Read each sentence. Draw a picture that shows what the sentence means."

Dolch Sight Word Activities

Name _____

two _____

into _____

again _____

been _____

want _____

a	a	a	b	e	e	g	i	i	n	n
n	n	o	o	t	t	t	w	w		

Directions: Tell the children, "Copy each of the words on the line next to the word."

Optional Activity: Tell the children, "Cut out the letters at the bottom of the page. Use the letters to make the words. Then glue each word on the line beside the printed word."

Dolch **Sight Word Activities**

Name

want

__ a __ t

w __ n __

been

__ b __ n

__ ee __

two

__ __

__ w __

__ o

into

in __ __

__ __ to

again

__ ag __

__ ain

Directions: Tell the children, "Say each word printed in dark type. Fill in the missing letters."

Dolch Sight Word Activities

Name _____

been
want
into
again
two

1. Do you _____ to eat the fish?

   _____ ?

2. Did the man read the book _____

   _____ to see the old house?

3. Have you _____

   _____ children for the book?

4. Did you thank the _____

   _____ the house to get his toys.

5. The boy went _____

Directions: Tell the children, "Read the words in dark print. Then read the incomplete sentences. Find the word in dark print that correctly completes each sentence. Then write that word in the blank."

Dolch **Sight Word Activities**

Name _____

PARENTS: Listen to your child read the sentences on this page and put a check mark beside each sentence that is read without error. Then display the paper in a prominent place. If your child has difficulty with any sentence, read the sentence to the child, pointing to each word as you read. Ask the child to read the sentence in the same way. Repeat this procedure several times.

☐ Did you see the play about the children who have a fish that can sing?

☐ Where have the two little children been?

☐ Has the boy been here again to play with your cat?

☐ Do you want to go into that old house with me again?

☐ I want two toys that will go into my wagon for my birthday.

☐ Have you been to see the funny show again?

Directions: Tell the children, "Learn to read the sentences, then take them home to read to your parents."

Dalch **Sight Word Activities**

Name _____

Directions: Tell the children, "Read each sentence below. Say the new word printed in dark print. Then say its letters. Repeat the word. Now trace the word with your pencil." Point out to the children that the word **live** has two pronunciations, /līv/ and /lĭv/.

I got a **new** ring for my birthday.

new

Will you **buy** me a new wagon?

buy

Do **many** children like to read a funny book?

many

Are any of **those** your toys?

those

Where do you **live**?

live

Dolch **Sight Word Activities**

Name _____

Directions: Tell the children, "Draw a line from each word that begins with a capital letter to the same word that begins with a small letter."

Live

Buy

Those

Many

New

many

those

new

buy

live

Mother will buy
me a new ball.

Many fish live
in the water.

Directions: Tell the children, "Read each sentence. Draw a picture that shows what the sentence means."

Dolch **Sight Word Activities**

Name _____

_____ buy

_____ new

_____ those

_____ many

_____ live

a	b	e	e	e	h	i	l	m	n
o	s	t	u	v	w	y	y		

Directions: Tell the children, "Copy each of the words on the line next to the word."

Optional Activity: Tell the children, "Cut out the letters at the bottom of the page. Use the letters to make the words. Then glue each word on the line beside the printed word."

Dolch **Sight Word Activities**

Name _____

new

_ e _ _ _

_ _ _ w

buy

b _ _ _

_ _ _ y

those

t _ o _ e

_ _ _ hos _

many

_ _ a _ y

m _ n _ _

live

l i _ _

_ _ _ ve

Dolch **Sight Word Activities**

Name _____

new
buy
those
many
live

1. How _____ fish can you eat?

2. Those children _____ near the school.

3. Did you buy a _____ doll for the girl?

4. Mother will _____ me those two new toys.

5. _____ chickens like to run around in the grass.

Directions: Tell the children, "Read the words in dark print. Then read the incomplete sentences. Find the word in dark print that correctly completes each sentence. Then write that word in the blank. Use a capital letter at the beginning of a sentence."

Dolch **Sight Word Activities**

Name _____

PARENTS: Listen to your child read the sentences on this page and put a check mark beside each sentence that is read without error. Then display the paper in a prominent place. If your child has difficulty with any sentence, read the sentence to the child, pointing to each word as you read. Ask the child to read the sentence in the same way. Repeat this procedure several times.

☐ Can we buy those
eight fish to eat?

☐ Would you like to buy one
of those new toys?

☐ Many of those children
have been to the
new school.

☐ Many children live
in the new house.

☐ I will buy a new wagon
for those children who
live down by the bus stop.

☐ Will you buy a new house
for the puppy to live in?

Directions: Tell the children, "Learn to read the sentences, then take them home to read to your parents."

Dolch Sight Word Activities

Name _____

Directions: Tell the children, "Read the word that goes with the picture. Then say its letters. Repeat the word. Now trace the word with your pencil."

Directions: Tell the children, "Read each sentence below. Say the new word printed in dark print. Then say its letters. Repeat the word. Now trace the word with your pencil."

A ring is **always** round. always

Always do your **best**. best

How **long** are you going to be here? long

Did you **give** some cake to Mother? give

four 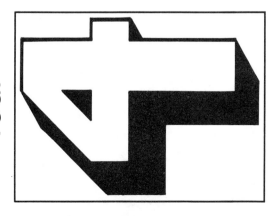 four

Name _____

Directions: Tell the children, "Draw a line from each word that begins with a capital letter to the same word that begins with a small letter."

Always

Give

Four

Best

Long

four

always

best

long

give

This long bus always has that old man on it.

The boy will run the best of all the children there.

Directions: Tell the children, "Read each sentence. Draw a picture that shows what the sentence means."

Dolch **Sight Word Activities**

Name _____

give _____

four _____

long _____

always _____

best _____

a	a	b	e	e	f	g	g	i	i	l
o	o	n	r	s	s	t	u	v	w	y

Directions: Tell the children, "Copy each of the words on the line next to the word."

Optional Activity: Tell the children, "Cut out the letters at the bottom of the page. Use the letters to make the words. Then glue each word on the line beside the printed word."

Dolch **Sight Word Activities**

Name _____

long

l ___ g

___ on

four

f ___ r

___ ou ___

best

b ___ s ___

___ e ___ t

give

g ___ e

___ iv ___

always

___ ways

al ___ ys

Directions: Tell the children, "Say each word printed in dark type. Fill in the missing letters."

Dalch **Sight Word Activities**

Name _____

best	
four	
always	
long	
give	

1. _____ _____ of those toys are mine.

2. Do you _____ say **thank you?**

3. A fish is at its _____ in the water.

4. Does it take _____ to clean up that wagon?

5. _____ the pretty ring to the little girl by the table.

Directions: Tell the children, "Read the words in dark print. Then read the incomplete sentences. Find the word in dark print that correctly completes each sentence. Then write that word in the blank. Use a capital letter at the beginning of a sentence."

Dolch **Sight Word Activities**

Name _____

PARENTS: Listen to your child read the sentences on this page and put a check mark beside each sentence that is read without error. Then display the paper in a prominent place. If your child has difficulty with any sentence, read the sentence to the child, pointing to each word as you read. Ask the child to read the sentence in the same way. Repeat this procedure several times.

☐ Please take this fish to my house and give it to my mother.

☐ Always do your best when you are at school.

☐ I always try to thank those who help me out.

☐ Four of our best chickens have run away.

☐ Give the long table to the school.

☐ It is always best to keep your house clean and pretty.

Directions: Tell the children, "Learn to read the sentences, then take them home to read to your parents."

Dalch Sight Word Activities

Name _____

Directions: Tell the children, "Read the word that goes with the picture. Then say its letters. Repeat the word. Now trace the word with your pencil."

Directions: Tell the children, "Read each sentence below. Say the new word printed in dark print. Then say its letters. Repeat the word. Now trace the word with your pencil."

Please try to come to see us **soon.**   soon

Is the school **open** at eight?   open

Does that wagon **work?**   work

Is my house **as** far away **as** your house?   as

ten   ten

Unit 45

Matching and Visualization 2

Name _____

Directions: Tell the children, "Draw a line from each word that begins with a capital letter to the same word that begins with a small letter."

As

Open

Ten

Soon

Work

work

soon

open

ten

as

There is an open
house at school.

Ten big chickens
eat at the
blue table.

Directions: Tell the children, "Read each sentence. Draw a picture that shows what the sentence means."

Dolch **Sight Word Activities**

Name _____

_____

_____ soon

as _____

_____

work _____ ten

_____

open _____

a	e	e	k	n	n	n	o	o
o	o	p	r	s	s	s	t	w

Directions: Tell the children, "Copy each of the words on the line next to the word."

Optional Activity: Tell the children, "Cut out the letters at the bottom of the page. Use the letters to make the words. Then glue each word on the line beside the printed word."

Dolch **Sight Word Activities**

Name _____

ten

n _ _ _

e _ _ _

soon

s _ _ _

oo _ _ _

as

_ _ _ _

open

_ _ _ _

op _ _ _

_ _ en _ _

work

_ _ rk _ _

wo _ _ _

Dolch **Sight Word Activities**

Name _____

as
work
soon
ten
open

1. _____ you and I will get to play house.

2. My mother will go to _____ today.

3. I will be there _____ soon as I can.

4. _____ little children will sit on the grass and fish.

5. Is the new school _____ ?

Directions: Tell the children, "Read the words in dark print. Then read the incomplete sentences. Find the word in dark print that correctly completes each sentence. Then write that word in the blank. Use a capital letter at the beginning of a sentence."

Dolch Sight Word Activities

Name _____

PARENTS: Listen to your child read the sentences on this page and put a check mark beside each sentence that is read without error. Then display the paper in a prominent place. If your child has difficulty with any sentence, read the sentence to the child, pointing to each word as you read. Ask the child to read the sentence in the same way. Repeat this procedure several times.

☐ Get to work as soon as you can today because it is going to rain.

☐ After school, we will give the ten children much work to do.

☐ Will the new school open soon?

☐ My father has to go to work as soon as it is light.

☐ At ten, Mother will hold an open house.

☐ As soon as you can work on it, please clean the old wagon.

Directions: Tell the children, "Learn to read the sentences, then take them home to read to your parents."

Dolch **Sight Word Activities**

Name _____

Directions: Tell the children, "Read the word that goes with the picture. Then say its letters. Repeat the word. Now trace the word with your pencil."

Directions: Tell the children, "Read each sentence below. Say the new word printed in dark print. Then say its letters. Repeat the word. Now trace the word with your pencil."

The fish we **ate** was very good.   ate

The table and chair are **black**.   black

Do **both** of them want to eat here?   both

There **were** three fish in the water.   were

three

three

Name

Directions: Tell the children, "Draw a line from each word that begins with a capital letter to the same word that begins with a small letter."

three

both

were

black

ate

Ate

Black

Both

Three

Were

The little black ball is on the long table.

Three chickens were by the blue house.

Directions: Tell the children, "Read each sentence. Draw a picture that shows what the sentence is about."

Name _____

three _____

were _____

ate _____

black _____

both _____

a	a	b	b	c	e	e	e	e	e	h
h	k	l	o	r	r	t	t	t	w	

Directions: Tell the children, "Copy each of the words on the line next to the word."

Optional Activity: Tell the children, "Cut out the letters at the bottom of the page. Use the letters to make the words. Then glue each word next to the printed word."

Dolch **Sight Word Activities**

Name _____

three

_____ _ _ _ ree

thr _____ _ _ _ _____

both

bo _____ _ _ _ _____

_____ a _ _ _ th _____

were

_____ w _ r _____

_____ e _ _ e _____

black

bla _____ _ _ _ _____

_____ _ _ _ ack

Directions: Tell the children, "Say each word printed in dark type. Fill in the missing letters."

Dolch Sight Word Activities

Name _____

ate
black
both
were
three

1. The man _ _ _ _ _ _ _ _ _ _ all the fish.

2. _____ children know how to make toys.

3. _____ the boy and girl were in school.

4. Give the _____ ring back to him now.

5. The three toys _____ under the red wagon.

Directions: Tell the children, "Read the words in dark print. Then read the incomplete sentences. Find the word in dark print that correctly completes each sentence. Then write that word in the blank. Use a capital letter at the beginning of a sentence."

Dalch Sight Word Activities

Name _____

□ Both black fish were far off into the water.

□ Three toys were in the grass for the children to play with.

□ The three children ate yellow cake together at the new long table today.

□ Their old black table and chair were both in the school play.

□ Mother and Father were going to pick up toys for the three children.

□ Both the boy and the girl were going to take the bus to see the show.

Dolch **Sight Word Activities**

Name _____

Directions: Tell the children, "Read each sentence below. Say the new word printed in dark print. Then say its letters. Repeat the word. Now trace the word with your pencil."

Where was this doll **made**?
made

What have you **done** with my new wagon?
done

That man **ran** by my house today.
ran

Every chair and desk in our school is black.
Every

What **shall** I do with this ring?
shall

Dolch **Sight Word Activities**

Name _____

Directions: Tell the children, "Draw a line from each word that begins with a capital letter to the same word that begins with a small letter."

Made	done
Shall	ran
Every	made
Ran	shall
Done	every

Father has made me three toys for my birthday.

The squirrel ran up the walk to the red school house.

Directions: Tell the children, "Read each sentence. Draw a picture that shows what the sentence is about."

Dolch **Sight Word Activities**

Name _____

_____ made

_____ every

_____ done

_____ ran

_____ shall

a	a	a	d	d	e	e	e	e	h	l
l	l	m	n	n	o	o	r	r	s	v	y

Directions: Tell the children, "Copy each of the words on the line next to the word."

Optional Activity: Tell the children, "Cut out the letters at the bottom of the page. Use the letters to make the words. Then glue each word next to the printed word."

Dalch Sight Word Activities

Name _____

shall

___ all

sha ___ ___

done

___ on ___

d ___ e

ran

___ a ___

___ ___ n

every

ev ___ y

___ ery

made

___ ad ___

m ___ d ___

Directions: Tell the children, "Say each word printed in dark type. Fill in the missing letters."

Dolch Sight Word Activities

Name _____

done
every
ran
shall
made

1. I like _____ _____ book I open.

2. The girl _____ fast to get to work.

3. What _____ I tell Father?

4. Look at what I _____ _____ in school today!

5. The boy will be _____ with my elephant book today.

Directions: Tell the children, "Read the words in dark print. Then read the incomplete sentences. Find the word in dark print that correctly completes each sentence. Then write that word in the blank."

Unit 47

Dolch **Sight Word Activities**

Name _____

PARENTS: Listen to your child read the sentences on this page and put a check mark beside each sentence that is read without error. Then display the paper in a prominent place. If your child has difficulty with any sentence, read the sentence to the child, pointing to each word as you read. Ask the child to read the sentence in the same way. Repeat this procedure several times.

Every round table in
our house was made by
Father and me.

Shall we run to the bus
stop so we don't get cold?

Is the boy done
with my wagon?

I shall give every doll I
have a ride in my wagon.

I made the little cake
by myself and when it
was done I ate it all.

The man made a new
ring for the birthday girl.

Directions: Tell the children, "Learn to read the sentences, then take them home to read to your parents."

Dolch **Sight Word Activities**

Name _____

Directions: Tell the children, "Read each sentence below. Say the new word printed in dark print. Then say its letters. Repeat the word. Now trace the word with your pencil."

Mother **gave** all ten children new toys.   gave

Once I saw a monkey ride an elephant.   Once

Which puppy will we **wash** first?   wash

What will Father **say** about the chair that we got?   say

We will **just** laugh when we see the funny play.   just

Dolch Sight Word Activities

Name _____

Directions: Tell the children, "Draw a line from each word that begins with a capital letter to the same word that begins with a small letter."

The girl gave the
fish to the little
black cat.

The boy will wash
the blue bus with
hot water.

Gave   once

Just   say

Once   wash

Wash   just

Say   gave

Directions: Tell the children, "Read each sentence. Draw a picture that shows what the sentence is about."

Dolch **Sight Word Activities**

Name _____

_____

_____

gave

_____

_____

once

_____

wash

_____

say

_____

just

a	a	c	e	g	h	j	n	o
s	s	s	t	u	v	w	y	

Directions: Tell the children, "Copy each of the words on the line next to the word."

Optional Activity: Tell the children, "Cut out the letters at the bottom of the page. Use the letters to make the words. Then glue each word next to the printed word."

Dolch **Sight Word Activities**

Name _____

once

c e _____

o__ __ s _____

say

a _____

_ _ s _____

gave

g a _____

_ _ v e _____

just

j _ s _____

_ u _ t _____

wash

w _ _ h _____

_ _ a s _ _____

Directions: Tell the children, "Say each word printed in dark type. Fill in the missing letters."

Dolch **Sight Word Activities**

Name _____

just
gave
once
say
wash

1. What did you _ _ _ _ _ _ _ _ ?

2. Did he help you _____ the wagon?

3. I _____ my ring to my mother to keep.

4. Can we play with the little puppy _____ this once?

5. _ _ _ _ _ _ _ _ I got to buy a new book just for myself.

Directions: Tell the children, "Read the words in dark print. Then read the incomplete sentences. Find the word in dark print that correctly completes each sentence. Then write that word in the blank. Use a capital letter at the beginning of a sentence."

Dolch **Sight Word Activities**

Name _____

PARENTS: Listen to your child read the sentences on this page and put a check mark beside each sentence that is read without error. Then display the paper in a prominent place. If your child has difficulty with any sentence, read the sentence to the child, pointing to each word as you read. Ask the child to read the sentence in the same way. Repeat this procedure several times.

☐ Once I gave my father the best book I could buy for his birthday.

☐ May I hold the little squirrel just once?

☐ What will Mother say if we wash up and go to sleep?

☐ The little girl just gave me some of her milk to drink.

☐ Did your father say that he once got hurt in a fall?

☐ The man ran from the bus stop to the well just once after work.

Directions: Tell the children, "Learn to read the sentences, then take them home to read to your parents."

Dolch **Sight Word Activities**

Name _____

Directions: Tell the children, "Read each sentence below. Say the new word printed in dark print. Then say its letters. Repeat the word. Now trace the word with your pencil."

I **came** here to see the play.

come

Did you and Mother **make** the cake together?

make

The new girl in school put her doll **upon** that table.

upon

My puppy is very **small**, but it is my very own.

small

Are you all **right**?

right

Name

Directions: Tell the children, "Draw a line from each word that begins with a capital letter to the same word that begins with a small letter."

make

came

right

upon

small

Right

Upon

Small

Make

Came

Father will make
a small cake
for Mother.

The boy came in
from the cold with
a small squirrel.

Directions: Tell the children, "Read each sentence. Draw a picture that shows what the sentence is about."

Dolch **Sight Word Activities**

Name _____

small _____ _ _ _ _ _ _ _ _ _ _ _

upon _____ _ _ _ _ _ _ _ _ _ _ _

make _____ _ _ _ _ _ _ _ _ _ _ _

came _____ _ _ _ _ _ _ _ _ _ _ _

right _____

a	a	a	c	g	h	e	e	k	i	l
l	m	m	m	n	o	p	r	s	t	u

Directions: Tell the children, "Copy each of the words on the line next to the word."

Optional Activity: Tell the children, "Cut out the letters at the bottom of the page. Use the letters to make the words. Then glue each word next to the printed word."

Dolch **Sight Word Activities**

Name _____

small

sma _____ _ _ _ _ _____

_____ a _____ ll

upon

_____ _ _ _ _ _____ on

up _____

came

_____ _ _ _ _ a _____ e

c _____ m

right

ri _____ _ _ _ _ t

_____ _ _ _ _ ght

make

_____ _ _ _ _ ke

ma _____ t

Dalch Sight Word Activities

Unit 49

Sentence Completion 5

Name _____

upon	
came	
make	
small	
right	

1. Is it all _____ if I go to see the play now?

2. Clean off this doll to _____ it pretty.

3. The show was "Once _____ a Bus Ride."

4. An elephant is big, but a puppy is _____.

5. Father and Mother _____ to see our show.

Directions: Tell the children, "Read the words in dark print. Then read the incomplete sentences. Find the word in dark print that correctly completes each sentence. Then write that word in the blank."

Dolch Sight Word Activities

Name _____

PARENTS: Listen to your child read the sentences on this page and put a check mark beside each sentence that is read without error. Then display the paper in a prominent place. If your child has difficulty with any sentence, read the sentence to the child, pointing to each word as you read. Ask the child to read the sentence in the same way. Repeat this procedure several times.

☐ As the boy was going to school, he came upon a small puppy.

☐ She got the small cat and put it right in the house.

☐ We came here to make a small birthday cake for Mother.

☐ When you get to the green light, walk to the right to get to my house.

☐ Will Father make us a small wagon to carry our toys in?

☐ The girl came to our house to play with me and my new red wagon.

Directions: Tell the children, "Learn to read the sentences, then take them home to read to your parents."

Dolch **Sight Word Activities**

Name _____

Directions: Tell the children, "Read each sentence below. Say the new word printed in dark print. Then say its letters. Repeat the word. Now trace the word with your pencil."

What **goes** up must come down.

goes

Six children ate **six** fish.

Six

First she made the cake, **then** she ate it.

then

He is the **only** boy in the house who is ten.

only

This water is not very **warm** or very clean.

warm

Name _____

Directions: Tell the children, "Draw a line from each word that begins with a capital letter to the same word that begins with a small letter."

Goes

Then

Six

Warm

Only

six

only

warm

then

goes

Six children will sing to the birthday girl.

The boy can only hold one warm puppy.

Directions: Tell the children, "Read each sentence. Draw a picture that shows what the sentence is about."

Dalch **Sight Word Activities**

Name _____

_____

warm _____

_____

then _____

goes _____

only _____

six _____

a	e	e	g	h	i	l	m	n	n	o
o	o	r	s	s	t	w	x	y		

Directions: Tell the children, "Copy each of the words on the line next to the word."

Optional Activity: Tell the children, "Cut out the letters at the bottom of the page. Use the letters to make the words. Then glue each word next to the printed word."

Dolch **Sight Word Activities**

Name _____

warm

w ___ m

___ ar ___

six

___ x

s ___

then

___ en

th ___

goes

g ___ s

___ oe ___

only

on ___

___ ly

Dolch **Sight Word Activities**

Name _____

only
then
six
goes
warm

1. Is it too _ _ _ _ _ _____ in the house?

2. There is _____ _ _ _ _ one squirrel in the grass.

3. First I will wash up, _____ _ _ _ _ I can eat.

4. The boy _____ _ _ _ _ to sleep only when it is warm.

5. Can _ _ _ _ _____ chickens sing "Am I Blue"?

Directions: Tell the children, "Read the words in dark print. Then read the incomplete sentences. Find the word in dark print that correctly completes each sentence. Then write that word in the blank. Use a capital letter at the beginning of a sentence."

Name _____

PARENTS: Listen to your child read the sentences on this page and put a check mark beside each sentence that is read without error. Then display the paper in a prominent place. If your child has difficulty with any sentence, read the sentence to the child, pointing to each word as you read. Ask the child to read the sentence in the same way. Repeat this procedure several times.

☐ The boy goes out to play
and then he goes right
into the house again.

☐ Our puppy and their
black cat get warm when
they play in the grass.

☐ Some of the six children
do not like warm milk;
they like only cold milk.

☐ The water is only
a little warm today.

☐ Can only six children
ride in the open wagon?

☐ That is the only bus
that goes to my school.

Directions: Tell the children, "Learn to read the sentences, then take them home to read to your parents."

Answer Key

Dolch **Sight Word Activities** Volume 2

Unit 26, Lesson 5

1. pretty
2. cake
3. birthday
4. wish
5. draw

Unit 27, Lesson 5

1. fish
2. by
3. man
4. could
5. so

Unit 28, Lesson 5

1. myself
2. fly
3. be
4. When
5. old

Unit 29, Lesson 5

1. An
2. grow
3. elephant
4. children *or* elephant *or* squirrel
5. squirrel

Unit 30, Lesson 5

1. why
2. milk
3. Drink
4. toys *or* milk
5. his

Unit 31, Lesson 5

1. good
2. These *or* Seven
3. better
4. These *or* Seven
5. got

Unit 32, Lesson 5

1. first
2. start
3. blue
4. who
5. carry

Unit 33, Lesson 5

1. never
2. table
3. hurt
4. any
5. water

Unit 34, Lesson 5

1. doll
2. five *or* own
3. show
4. own
5. chickens

Unit 35, Lesson 5

1. well
2. yellow
3. walk
4. don't
5. hold *or* walk

Unit 36, Lesson 5

1. far
2. red *or* green
3. away
4. fall
5. green

Unit 37, Lesson 5

1. off
2. Try
3. very
4. call
5. their

Unit 38, Lesson 5
1. them
2. clean
3. but
4. Pick *or* Clean
5. They

Unit 39, Lesson 5
1. because
2. too
3. must *or* now
4. or
5. now

Unit 40, Lesson 5
1. full
2. One
3. pull
4. wagon
5. down

Unit 41, Lesson 5
1. Eight
2. Which
3. ring
4. use
5. round

Unit 42, Lesson 5
1. want
2. again
3. been
4. two
5. into

Unit 43, Lesson 5
1. many
2. live
3. new
4. buy
5. Those *or* Many

Unit 44, Lesson 5
1. Four
2. always
3. best
4. long
5. Give

Unit 45, Lesson 5
1. Soon
2. work
3. as
4. Ten *or* Soon
5. open

Unit 46, Lesson 5
1. ate
2. Both *or* Three
3. Both
4. black
5. were

Unit 47, Lesson 5
1. every
2. ran
3. shall
4. made
5. done

Unit 48, Lesson 5
1. say *or* wash
2. wash
3. gave
4. just
5. Once

Unit 49, Lesson 5
1. right
2. make
3. Upon
4. small
5. came

Unit 50, Lesson 5
1. warm
2. only
3. then
4. goes
5. six *or* warm *or* only

NOTES

NOTES

NOTES

NOTES